Books in the Linkers series

Homes discovered through Art & Technology
Homes discovered through Geography
Homes discovered through History
Homes discovered through Science

Toys discovered through Art & Technology
Toys discovered through Geography
Toys discovered through History
Toys discovered through Science

Myself discovered through Art & Technology
Myself discovered through Geography
Myself discovered through History
Myself discovered through Science

Water discovered through Art & Technology
Water discovered through Geography
Water discovered through History
Water discovered through Science

First paperback edition 1996
First published 1996 in hardback by A&C Black (Publishers) Limited
35 Bedford Row, London WC1R 4JH

ISBN 0-7136-4600-4
A CIP catalogue record for this book is available from the British Library.

Commissioned photographs by Zul Mukhida
Design by Jean Wheeler

Acknowledgements

The publishers would like to thank the following people and organizations for supplying some of the toys used in this book: The Early Learning Centre, Swindon; 13 (right), Mr and Mrs W.W. Bryant; cover, 3, 9 (both), 10 (both), 11, 12 (both), 23 (both).
Picture acknowledgements: Beamish, The North of England Open Air Museum; 20 (left), Robert Opie; 2 (left), 4, 5 (left), 6, 7 (top), 8, 14 (both), 15, 16 (both), 18 (both), 19, 21 (both), Positive Images; 2 (right), 13 (left).

Printed and bound in Italy by L.E.G.O.

Toys

discovered through

History

Karen Bryant-Mole

Contents

A & C Black • London

Toys from the past

Children have always played with toys.

Your mum and dad, your grandparents, your great-grandparents and even your great-great-grandparents played with toys when they were young.

a 1930s doll's tea-party

a 1960s doll

This book will show you some of the toys they might have played with.
Some of the toys, like this doll, look very similar to toys that can be bought today.
Other toys look very different.

This toy concrete mixer was made during the 1940s. That means it is more than fifty years old.

a 1940s concrete mixer

A year is the amount of time that there is from one birthday to the next.
A year probably seems like a very long time to you.

But, some of the toys in this book are more than one hundred years old.

Jigsaws

The very first jigsaw puzzles were maps that were stuck onto thin pieces of wood and then cut into pieces. Whoever was doing the puzzle had to put the map back together again.

Bible stories

Many early jigsaw puzzles showed pictures of stories from the Bible.
On Sundays, many children were only allowed to play with toys that were to do with the Bible.

a 1900s jigsaw puzzle

Pictures

Jigsaws have always used the idea of putting a picture back together. However, the pictures used for jigsaws have changed a lot over the years.

Here is a jigsaw that was made when trains were powered by steam.

a 1970s puzzle

a 1930s jigsaw puzzle

This jigsaw shows the type of clothes people wore in the 1970s.

Looking at the pictures on old jigsaws can tell us a lot about the way people lived.

Cars

Almost as soon as cars appeared on the roads, children wanted to play with toy cars.

These toy cars were made to look as much like the real thing as possible.

Tinplate
The first toy cars were often made from tinplate.

The car below has a chauffeur. Years ago, there were very few cars and only very rich people could afford them.

They sometimes paid chauffeurs to drive them around.

a 1920s tinplate toy car

a 1940s toy vehicle catalogue

Catalogues

As new designs in real cars were introduced, they were copied in the toy cars.
Toy manufacturers produced catalogues, like the one above, to show people the cars and other vehicles that they made.

Now

This is a modern toy car.
You might see cars like this on today's busy roads.

a 1990s toy car

Dolls

The first dolls were often made of wood.
They usually had painted faces and sometimes
had painted clothes, too.

Porcelain

Many dolls were made from a type
of pottery called porcelain.
Sometimes the porcelain had
a shiny coating.
This was called glazed china.
Porcelain that wasn't shiny
was called bisque.

an 1880s bisque doll

Sailor doll

This doll was made from felt.
The sailor's eyes and mouth were painted onto the felt.
Passengers on big ships bought dolls like this as gifts and souvenirs.

a 1920s felt doll

Shirley Temple

Shirley Temple was a famous child actress. This doll was made to look like her.

a 1930s composition doll

The doll was made from composition, which was a mixture of either sawdust and glue or paper and glue.

Most of today's dolls are made from a soft plastic, called vinyl.

Dolls' houses

Dolls' houses often copied the style of real houses that were being built at that time.

Hand-made houses
This dolls' house was made by hand.
It was a type of house known as a town house.

a 1910s town house

Suburban houses
Later, real houses like this were built on the outskirts of towns, in areas called suburbs. Your grandmother might have played with a dolls' house like this.

a 1930s suburban house

Furniture

Inside, the dolls' houses were usually decorated in a similar way to children's own homes. The furniture looked like small versions of the furniture children saw all around them.

Dolls' houses can help to show us what people's homes looked like in the past.

Pretend play

Children sometimes like to copy the things that they see grown-ups doing.

a 1910s tea set

Tea-time
Your great-grandmother could have used a china tea-set like this for dolls' tea parties.

Grown-ups used real tea-sets for their tea parties.

Washing clothes
Before people had washing machines, they washed their clothes by hand.
This toy washing set looks just like one that a grown-up would have used.

a 1920s washing set

Dolls' prams

Lots of children have pushed dolls around in prams and pretended the dolls were their babies.

a 1960s doll's pram

a 1990s toy telephone

Telephone

This is a toy telephone.
It has push-buttons, just like today's modern phones.

All these toys show pretend versions of real life objects that were in use when the toys were made.

Table-top games

Before television was invented, families used to spend more time together playing games.

Card games

Card games were very popular. Snap was played by both children and adults.

This pack is described as 'A Most Amusing Game for Evening Parties'.

a 1920s game

a 1910s game

Blow Football

In this game, the little ball had to be placed in the middle of the table. The players had to blow down tubes, trying to blow the ball past the goal posts.

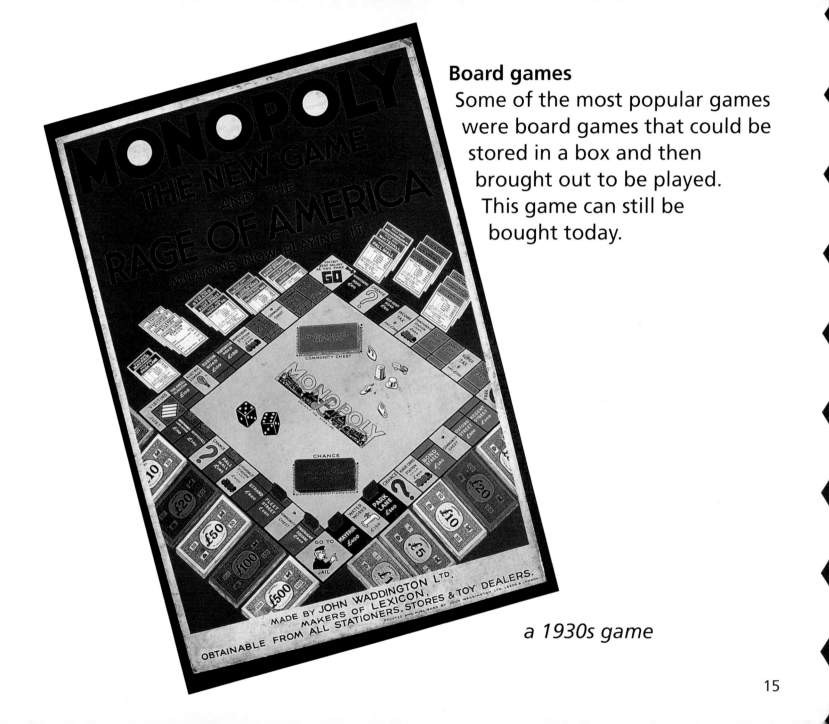

Board games

Some of the most popular games were board games that could be stored in a box and then brought out to be played. This game can still be bought today.

a 1930s game

Moving toys

The first moving toys had to be pushed or pulled.
Later, other ways of making them move
were invented.

Clockwork
This clockwork toy had
a key which was used
to wind up a spring
inside the toy.
As the spring
unwound it turned
cogs which made
the horses move
and made the doll
turn her head.

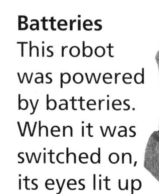

Batteries
This robot
was powered
by batteries.
When it was
switched on,
its eyes lit up
and it moved its arms and legs.
Your father might have had a toy
like this.

Radio control

This modern car is worked by using a control unit. Radio waves pass between the control unit and car. The car can move in different directions. Batteries are needed to power both the car and the control unit.

a 1960s battery-operated toy

a 1990s radio-controlled toy

Train sets

The first toy trains were made soon after the first real trains began to run.

an 1880s carpet train

Carpet trains

Early toy trains, like the one above, were known as 'carpet' trains because they ran across the floor and not along tracks.
Some of these trains had to be pushed or pulled.
Others went by themselves, worked by steam, like real trains, or by clockwork.

Tracks

Later, toy trains were made to run along tracks.
Clockwork trains like the one in this picture, did not run for very long before the clockwork ran down.
Steam trains were messy and difficult to work. The hot steam could be dangerous, too.

a 1920s clockwork train

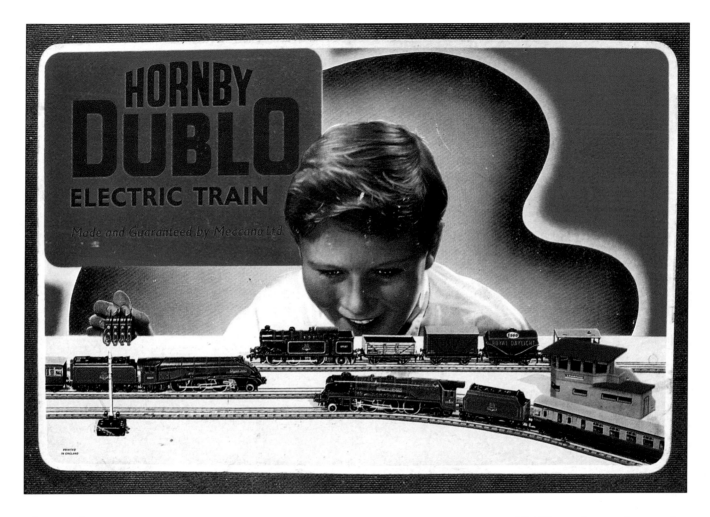

a 1960s electric train

Electric trains

Trains then began to be powered by electricity.
This meant that the trains could keep running
until the power was switched off.

Outdoor toys

Some toys are usually played with outside in the fresh air.

Marbles

Children have played with marbles for thousands of years.
The idea is to try to win some of your friends' marbles
without losing any of your own.

*children playing
marbles in the 1910s*

1900s spinning tops

Spinning tops

Spinning tops came in lots of shapes and sizes.

To spin a top, you wind a piece of string around the spindle, then throw the top to the ground, holding onto the end of the string. The top starts to spin as it flies through the air and keeps on spinning when it lands.

Skipping

Skipping ropes used to be simple pieces of rope. Later they were made with wooden handles. Today's skipping ropes come in lots of bright colours.

a 1940s skipping rope

21

Teddy bears

In 1892, the president of America, Theodore Roosevelt, caught a baby bear. The president's nick-name was Teddy.
A toymaker called one of his bears, Teddy's Bear. Soon, the name 'teddy bear' was used for all toy bears.

The first bears
Early bears had very long arms and pointed snouts. Their noses and mouths were sewn in black thread and they usually had glass or button eyes.

a 1900s bear

Noisy bears
Some bears growl when they are tipped backwards. Others, like the teddy on the right, have a squeaker that makes a noise when it is pressed.

Collectors

Some people collect teddy bears. Some teddies, like this German bear, can become quite valuable.

a 1990s bear

a 1940s bear

Many grown-ups still have the teddy they played with when they were children.
Teddies are very special toys.

Glossary

china a type of pottery
cogs a set of notched wheels that connect together
invent think of or make something new
manufacturers companies that make something
snout an animal's nose
souvenirs things that people buy to remind them of a time or a place

spindle a rod or pin that sometimes looks a bit like a stalk
tinplate a metal made by coating a thin sheet of steel with an even thinner layer of tin
valuable worth a lot of money
vehicles machines used for travel

Index

How to use this book

Each book in this series takes a familiar topic or theme and focuses on one area of the curriculum: science, art and technology, geography or history. The books are intended as starting points, illustrating some of the many different angles from which a topic can be studied. They should act as springboards for further investigation, activity or information seeking.

The following list of books may prove useful.

Further books to read

Series	Title	Author	Publisher
Changing Times	Toys and Games School	Ruth Thompson "	Watts
History from Objects	Toys	K. Bryant-Mole	Wayland
History from Photographs	Toys	Kath Cox & Pat Hughes	Wayland
History Mysteries	Toys	Tanner & Wood	A&C Black

Timeline

You can use this timeline to work out how long ago the toys in this book were made and to compare the ages of different toys.

nearly 120 years ago	nearly 110 years ago	nearly 100 years ago	nearly 90 years ago	nearly 80 years ago	nearly 70 years ago	nearly 60 years ago	nearly 50 years ago	nearly 40 years ago	nearly 30 years ago	nearly 20 years ago	nearly 10 years ago
the 1880s	the 1890s	the 1900s	the 1910s	the 1920s	the 1930s	the 1940s	the 1950s	the 1960s	the 1970s	the 1980s	the 1990s
1880	1890	1900	1910	1920	1930	1940	1950	1960	1970	1980	1990